JAN 2012

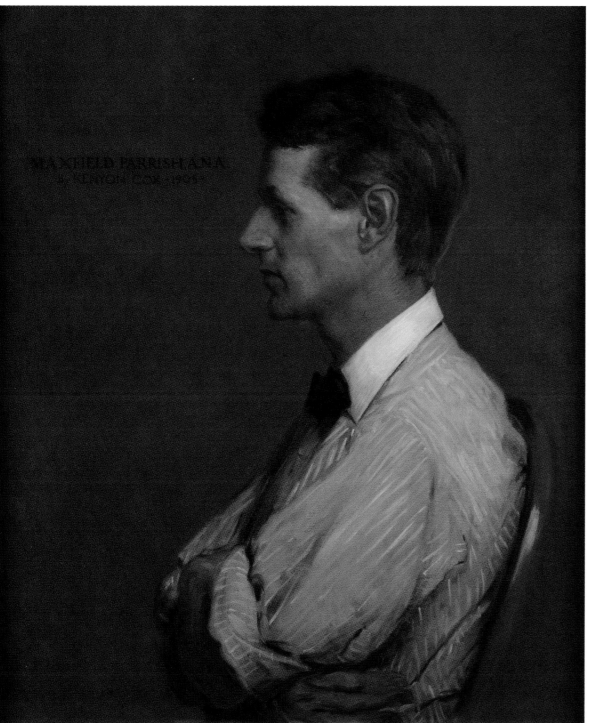

MAXFIELD PARRISH
PAINTER OF MAGICAL MAKE-BELIEVE

Maxfield Parrish, by Kenyon Cox

I woke up in the dark an' saw things standin' in a row, by Maxfield Parrish

MAXFIELD PARRISH

PAINTER OF MAGICAL MAKE-BELIEVE

Lois V. Harris

PELICAN PUBLISHING COMPANY

Gretna 2011

In memory of my grandmother Lillian Simpson,
who battled tuberculosis at Saranac Lake, New York,
like Maxfield Parrish, and went on to enjoy a long, lively life

The word "Pelican" and the depiction of a pelican
are trademarks of Pelican Publishing Company, Inc.,
and are registered in the U.S. Patent and Trademark Office.

Library of Congress Cataloging-in-Publication Data

Harris, Lois V.
    Maxfield Parrish : painter of magical make-believe / Lois V. Harris.
        p. cm.
    ISBN 978-1-4556-1472-1 (hardcover : alk. paper) 1. Parrish, Maxfield, 1870-1966—Juvenile literature.
2. Painters—United States—Biography—Juvenile literature. I. Parrish, Maxfield, 1870-1966. II. Title.
    ND237.P25213H37 2011
    759.13—dc22
    [B]
                                2011014767

Back-jacket illustration: *Florentine Fete* (detail), Maxfield Parrish, 1916, lithograph on paper, 8 5/8 x 14 1/8 inches, used by permission of the Free Library of Philadelphia, Rare Book Department.

Printed in Singapore
Published by Pelican Publishing Company, Inc.
1000 Burmaster Street, Gretna, Louisiana 70053

Dragon, by Maxfield Parrish

MAXFIELD PARRISH
PAINTER OF MAGICAL MAKE-BELIEVE

Fred's eyes sparkled on his third Christmas when he saw the pictures in his new sketchbook. His father, who was an artist, had filled the pages with drawings of funny animals and elves. Fred copied the pictures and practiced. By age seven, he drew wicked dragons for his friends.

Maxfield Parrish

Art-students and copyists in the Louvre gallery, Paris, by Winslow Homer

Frederick Parrish was born in Philadelphia, Pennsylvania on July 25, 1870. When he was fourteen, Fred and his parents, Elizabeth and Stephen Parrish, traveled to Europe. He attended school in Paris, France, and painted at his easel. With his father, he often visited the vast Louvre Museum. They watched artists copy famous paintings and sell their work to wealthy people.

Letter to Henry Bancroft, by Maxfield Parrish

Canterbury Cathedral from Christchurch Gate,
by Peter G. Livesey

For two years, the family toured Europe. Fred sent letters with amusing pictures to his cousin, Henry, and wrote about exploring ancient ruins, exciting cities, and splendid cathedrals. After returning to Philadelphia, Fred wanted to learn how to design and construct buildings. In 1888, he began studying architecture at nearby Haverford College.

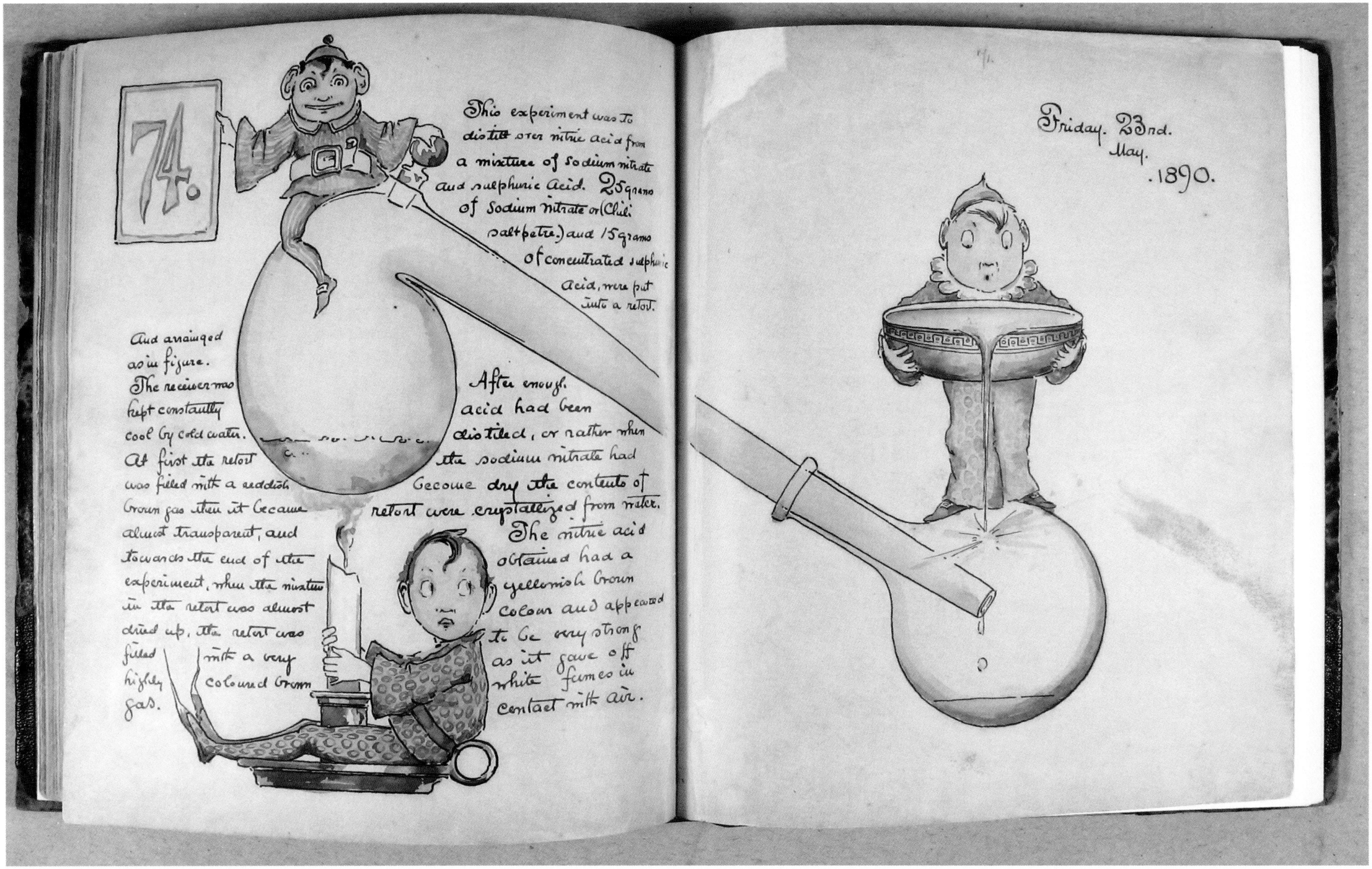

Chemistry Notebook, by Maxfield Parrish

The Copper Beech Tree on Founders Green,
by Charles F. Ward

Guitar, by Maxfield Parrish

Fred worked hard and received good grades. He decorated the walls of his room with chalk and crayon drawings, drew in notebooks, painted his guitar, and daydreamed while lying under the copper beech trees. Years later he said, "There were grand trees in those days, and grand trees do something to you."

Fred thought more and more about being an artist and longed to take art classes. The college did not offer any, so after two years, he left.

Maxfield Parrish

Old King Cole, by Maxfield Parrish

Fred enrolled at the Pennsylvania Academy of the Fine Arts in Philadelphia. While a student, he exhibited a landscape painting in an art show. He also earned his first commission by painting a picture and cartoon figures for the walls of a clubhouse.

Low Tide—Bay of Fundy, by Stephen Parrish

During the summers, Fred and his father painted land-scape pictures along the New England coast. Stephen Parrish was known for his etchings. Fred said his "papa" trained him to notice nature and was his best teacher.

Fred liked the sound of "Maxfield," his grandmother's family name, and began signing his name "M.P." or "Maxfield Parrish." Before long, almost everyone called him Maxfield.

At age twenty-five, Maxfield married Lydia Austin, an art teacher. Soon he sailed to Europe and visited the Louvre Museum again. He talked to artists copying the Old Masters' pictures and studied paintings hundreds of years old. "What an awesome feeling to be in such a presence," Maxfield wrote Lydia. "I dream about beautiful reds and blues and greens and glorious whites."

Lydia Austin Parrish

Maxfield returned home, created bold simple designs for ads and magazine illustrations, and won many poster contests. People praised his style and imagination.

Poster for P.A.F.A. Poster Show (1896), by Maxfield Parrish

The Oaks

In 1898, Lydia and Maxfield moved to Plainfield, New Hampshire. Near his parents' home, he and a carpenter built a small house among the trees. Maxfield named it "The Oaks" and wrote a friend, "Such an ideal country . . . a place to dream one's life away."

Solid Comfort, by S. R. Stoddard

But his happiness disappeared when his mother left his father and moved away. Then, Maxfield fell ill with tuberculosis. In those days, many people died from the lung disease, as scientists had not discovered a medicine to help them get well. Doctors advised him to stay outside in the cold air.

Lydia and Maxfield spent the winter at a mountain treatment center at Saranac Lake, New York. He needed money and painted outside. He shivered, working with one hand and sitting on the other to warm it. When his ink froze, he tried oil paints—they flowed. Maxfield loved their colors. After that, he usually worked with oils.

Photograph/Postcard of Tourists Playing Golf at the Resort at Castle Hot Springs (Ariz.)

The next winter, Lydia and Maxfield visited Castle Hot Springs, Arizona. A magazine paid his expenses for pictures of the Southwest. He painted and continued to recover, saying the desert shadows are "a blue from dreamland, a blue from which all the skies of the world were made."

Maxfield Parrish On Horseback

Maxfield's illustrations, painted in daring colors, won prizes from magazines. Printers invented a new way to copy paintings and made good cheap color copies of his art. One magazine sold thousands of his winning prints for ten cents each, earning him extra money.

December 1901 success Christmas number, by Maxfield Parrish

Maxfield also illustrated adult books, and children enjoyed his fantasyland pictures in storybooks.

The Fisherman and the Genie, by Maxfield Parrish

Sing a Song of Sixpence, by Maxfield Parrish

Maxfield painted large murals for businesses and homes and called it all "mighty good fun." In each picture, he included a glimpse of a landscape. Once he wrote a friend, "I've been looking forward to the day for years when I could do . . . landscapes mostly."

Ferry's Seeds: Mary, Mary Quite Contrary,
by Maxfield Parrish

PETER   PIPER

Peter Piper picked a peck of pickled pepper

USE

FERRY'S SEEDS

Meanwhile at "The Oaks," Maxfield and his carpenter friend added gardens, rooms, and a studio building. Sometimes his four children posed for him, or he painted himself.

Ferry's Seeds: Peter Piper, by Maxfield Parrish

The Adlake Camera, by Maxfield Parrish

Sometimes he painted the cat.

The King and Queen Might Eat Thereof and Noblemen Besides, by Maxfield Parrish

Maxfield's fanciful pictures decorated candy boxes, and an order sheet for his prints was tucked inside. People liked his art, bought the candy, and ordered thousands of his prints. Maxfield's art advertised more products, and the products sold. Soon his art appeared on calendars and cards. Printers copied more Parrish paintings. Print sales exploded, and his art brightened millions of homes.

In 1925, thousands of fans enjoyed Maxfield's paintings in a New York gallery show. They wondered how he made the colors glow. Maxfield said he never mixed his paints but brushed on many layers of pure color like the Old Masters. He added a coat of varnish to each layer and let the colors shine.

Princess Parizade Bringing Home the Singing Tree, by Maxfield Parrish

The deep shades of blue he created became known as "Parrish blue." When asked how he made it, Maxfield said it "is just ordinary blue you can buy around the corner, but what I put next to it is what makes it what it is."

The Lantern Bearers, by Maxfield Parrish

Irises, by Vincent van Gogh

Mont Sainte-Victoire, by Paul Cézanne

In his sixties, Maxfield agreed to do only landscapes for a calendar and card company. He exhibited his landscapes in 1936 in New York City. *Time* magazine said the three most popular print artists "in the world are van Gogh, Cézanne and Maxfield Parrish." But other art critics complained that his art looked too real, like a photograph.

Hill Top Farm, Winter,
by Maxfield Parrish

Maxfield went on painting—his way. For twenty-seven years, people bought calendars and cards with his scenes. He called them pictures of "a grand good place to be in."

After Lydia died in 1953, Maxfield continued painting at "The Oaks." He worked until he was ninety-one, when his shaking hands forced him to put down his brush. In 1964 and 1966, Maxfield's major art exhibitions drew crowds again— and his eyes twinkled. One critic said the public was "looking back at pictures by an old friend."

Maxfield died peacefully at "The Oaks" on March 30, 1966, at age ninety-five. A newspaper said, "He appeals to practically everyone." For the first time in history, an artist had created for more than a few. Maxfield Parrish painted a magical make-believe land for millions of people.

Maxfield Parrish

CREDITS